MAKING A NEW START

MAKING A NEW START

No Turning Back. Never Give Up. Refuse to Quit.

Jason Creech
Edited by Lisa Susong
and Helen Wilder

Making A New Start

Publisher: A Church Called Home
www.acch.us

ISBN: 979-8-684-99329-9

Acknowledgements

First and foremost, let me say how very thankful I am for our glorious God, His Son, and the daily inspiration of the Holy Spirit. Words could never express how grateful I am to my parents for always encouraging my brother and me to go after our dreams. My wife, Melissa, has been a champion of the faith. Her passion for Jesus inspires me and our kids. Thank you for being such an amazing wife! I know being a pastor's kid is not always easy, but our two children have made it look easy. Thank you Tori and Chaz for who you are.

Jennifer Kitts has done an incredible job with the publication of my books and I cannot thank her enough. Jennifer, you've been an answer to prayer for both Melissa and me. Thank you for doing such an amazing job. Karen Arnwine and Helen Wilder have proofread several books for me over the years; I appreciated you both. Lisa Susong did the editorial work on this book and Lisa, as always, you did a fantastic job.

A special thanks to our staff, our leaders, and the amazing team we have at A Church Called Home for making church so much fun.

Table of Contents

Welcome to the Journey

Thank you for picking up this little book. I wrote this especially for those who are making a new start by placing their faith in Christ. Opening your heart to Jesus and making Him the Lord of your life is absolutely the best decision you will ever make. When you're starting out, it can be helpful to have a fellow traveler along for the journey. That's what I hope to be to you over the next few days as we spend this time together.

This book was written to help you discover what Christ has done in your life, and at the same time, giving you some great next steps. As we make this journey together, I pray that you will be enlightened, encouraged, and empowered. My hope is that you will always stay firmly rooted in His love, His church, and His purpose. Let's get started!

- Pastor Jason

A New Start

For the first twenty years of my life, making a new start was never a challenge for me. Starting something new was always exciting. I didn't have a starting problem; I had a quitting problem. From an early age, giving up had become the theme of my life. I joined the Boy Scouts with great plans of becoming an Eagle Scout, but after a weekend of snipe hunting, a serious battle with poison ivy, and a sunken canoe, I quit! When the movie *Karate Kid* hit the box office in the mid 80's, my mind was made up. I would become the next Ralph Macchio. My mom signed me up at a local night club that served as a dojo on Tuesday nights. I broke my hand trying to break a board, so I quit! Little League Baseball wasn't any different. Two years of riding the bench was a waste of time, so to keep from breaking tradition, I quit!

Michael Jordan stirred something in my heart for basketball. My dad was kind enough to put up a ball goal at the end of our driveway. I won several back-to-back NBA titles playing solo games at that location. Then, the day came to try out for real. My first day at practice, we ran a layup drill; I shot 32 layups. Do you want to guess how many I made? Zero! Nada! I only hit the rim twice. Needless to say, I quit! Football and tennis were no different. I tried them both, and I quit them both.

The same was true academically. Somewhere around the fourth grade, I shut down. I gave up. Sixth grade was so much fun, I decided to repeat it. In high school, I failed biology, algebra and home economics. Yes, I took home economics in high school. The class was packed with girls, and I thought it would be an easy A; it ended up being an easy F.

The turning point for me was my senior year of high school. I was nineteen, and although I was young, my addictions were very real. One Sunday morning, my mom asked me to go to church with her. That was the day I heard the gospel in a way I had never heard it before. The following week, I prayed with the pastor, asking Jesus to forgive me, to free me of addiction, and to come into my life. That day was a game changer.

Even though I felt incredible, full of joy, and light as a feather, I still had my doubts. I didn't doubt God, but I sure doubted myself. Growing up, my question was never, "How do I get saved?" My question was, "How do I stay saved?" I believed salvation was somewhat God's responsibility, and more so, my responsibility. I totally believed it was His job to save me (once I confessed my sin); but from there my understanding of salvation was a little fuzzy. Even though I had never read the Bible (not even a verse), I had developed my own expert opinion of how salvation worked, and it looked something like this:

1. I go to Jesus and confess my sins.

2. Christ forgives me and cleanses me of my sins.

3. I keep myself clean and spotless before God, proving my love to Him.

4. If I keep myself spotless until death, God will allow me to enter Heaven.

Now, I'm going to get right to it here. If that's the gospel, the "*good news,*" then the good news is not good at all. You see, I know me, and I know there's no way by my own effort that I can live a perfect life before God. The very thought that I can prove my commitment to Him by sheer willpower is nothing short of religious arrogance and pride. The origin of sin is pride. Our Lord leaves no doubt concerning how He feels about pride: "*I resist the proud...*" (Proverbs 8:13).

But God's good news is nothing like my good news. My good news is not good news; it's bad news, but God's good news is great news. In this chapter, we are going to look at the Word of God together, with the goal of gaining a clear understanding of the gospel, the good news of Jesus Christ. I want to show you from Scripture what takes place when someone receives Christ into their life.

Let me begin with a statement that is not politically correct, but it is biblically correct: we are not born children of God. We were born sons and daughters of disobedience, children of wrath.

Let's look at this in Scripture:

> *And you were dead in the trespasses and sins in which you once walked, following the course of this world, following the prince of the power of the air, the spirit that is now at work in the sons of disobedience – among whom we all once lived in the passions of our flesh, carrying out the desires of the body and the mind, and were by nature children of wrath, like the rest of mankind.*
>
> — *Ephesians 2:1-3*

When you have children, you quickly realize that you don't have to teach them to do wrong; they will figure that out on their own. You do, however, have to teach them to do what is right. I have a preacher friend who often says, "If you don't believe in the devil, apparently you haven't had children yet." When you start having children, you soon discover that those sweet little angels will become quite the opposite if left to themselves. That's because we are born with a nature to sin (Colossians 3:5).

If we are not born children of God, how do we become children of God? The answer is in John chapter one. Notice the passage below:

Jesus came to His own, and His own people did not receive Him. But to all who did receive Him, who believed in His name, He gave them the right to become the children of God.

— *John 1:11-12*

When you turn to Jesus, confess your sins, and ask Him into your life, at that moment you become a child of God. Jesus referred to this as *being born again* (John 3:3). When a baby is born, the child has no past. When a person is born again, his or her past sins are remembered no more; the slate is wiped clean. Notice the verses below:

"Come now, let's settle this," says the LORD. *"Though your sins are like scarlet, I will make them as white as snow. Though they are red like crimson, I will make them as white as wool."*

— *Isaiah 1:18*

I – yes, I alone — will blot out your sins for My own sake and will never think of them again.

— *Isaiah 43:25*

Let's look again at Ephesians 2. Notice verses four through six:

But God, being rich in mercy, because of the great love with which He loved us, even when we were dead in our trespasses, made us alive together with Christ – by grace you have been saved – and raised us up with Him and seated us with Him in the heavenly places in Christ Jesus.

— Ephesians 2:4-6

I love the word *but* in the Bible. The word *but* in the Bible is like the word *void* on a check; it cancels out everything that came before it. Has anyone ever tried to apologize to you and then threw in the word *but*?

I am sorry for the way I acted, *but...*

I am sorry for what I said, *but...*

I don't think so! The word *but* in an apology cancels out any attempt to make things right.

Ephesians chapter two says that *we were born children of wrath, but God, being rich in mercy... made us alive together with Christ.*

Romans 6:23 says that *the wages of sin is death, but the gift of God is eternal life through Jesus Christ our Lord.* The enemy had a plan for your life, *but* God had a plan long before the devil did. God's plan for your life begins with you receiving the gift His Son offers you through His death and resurrection.

Let's talk about this gift for a moment. Romans 5:17 calls it the gift of righteousness. The word *righteous* means to be made right. Jesus made us right with God by canceling the debt our sins incurred (Colossians 2:18). We are made right with God the moment we place our faith in Christ and ask Him to forgive us of our sins. Look at Romans 3:

We are made right with God by placing our faith in Jesus Christ. And this is true for everyone who believes, no matter who we are. For everyone has sinned; we all fall short of God's glorious standard. Yet God, in His grace, freely makes us right in His sight. He did this through Christ Jesus when He freed us from the penalty for our sins. For God presented Jesus as the sacrifice for sin. People are made right with God when they believe that Jesus sacrificed His life, shedding His blood.

— Romans 3:22-25

If you have asked Jesus into your life, the following is true about you:

- You are no longer who you used to be (2 Corinthians 5:17).

- You are forgiven (Isaiah 43:25).

- You are clean (Isaiah 1:18).

- You are holy (1 Peter 2:9).

7

- You are chosen (1 Peter 2:9).

- Nothing can separate you from God's love (Romans 8:38).

- God has forgiven all your sins (Psalm 103:2).

- Jesus bore your sins in His body on the cross; therefore, you are dead to sin, and alive unto God (1 Peter 2:24, Romans 6:11, 2 Corinthians 5:21).

- You can win over any struggle (Romans 8:37).

- You can break free from any addiction (Romans 6:6).

- Whom the Son sets free, is free indeed (John 8:36).

Come on, praise God for that!

We are made right with God the moment we place our faith in Christ and ask Him to forgive us of our sins.

Don't let the devil tell you that nothing happened when you prayed the prayer of salvation. Don't let hell keep you from enjoying the new identity you now have as a child of God. One of the last things Jesus said in Scripture is recorded in Revelation 21:5. He said, *"Behold, I make all things new."* When you received Jesus in your life, He gave you a new start. This is a new day. Welcome to the new you!

Two Weeks Later

March 15, 1992 was the day I received Jesus. Words cannot express how amazing I felt after praying with my pastor that day. I knew the Lord had done something in my life. Then, two weeks later, I met up with some old friends, and I messed up big time. I sinned. I didn't make a mistake. I sinned. Mistakes are accidental. Sin is intentional. I made a choice. I sinned.

Until that time, I had become an expert at giving up. Now, for the first time in my life, I refused to quit. I refused to allow my sin to push me away from God. Instead of ignoring Him and hoping He hadn't seen my failure, I ran to Him.

A good indicator of spiritual maturity is how much time you allow to pass between the moment you mess up and the moment you run to Jesus. If the sin you committed three weeks ago has kept you distant, you have no idea who Jesus really is. Someone once asked the question, "If you were going to get caught in the worst moral moment of your life, who would you want to be caught by?" If your answer is anyone other than Jesus, you have a poor revelation of who Jesus is.

1 John 2:1 says, "*I write these things to you that you might not sin, but if anyone sins, we have an advocate with The Father, Jesus Christ the righteous. He is the propitiation for our sins.*" The word *propitiation* means, "the satisfaction of a debt." That's our Lord. That's Jesus! He satisfied once and for all, the debt our sins incurred. The Bible refers to Jesus as the Lamb of God, who *takes away* the sin of the world (John 1:29). I would go as far as to say that people who go to Hell don't go to Hell because of their sins; they go to Hell because they choose to pay for their sins. There is a place where you can pay for your sins, but it will take an eternity to pay off that debt. Jesus nailed our debt to the cross once and for all, freeing us of the charges held against us. Colossians 2:13-14 says that *we were dead because of our sins and because of our sinful nature. Then God made us alive with Christ, for He forgave all our sins. He canceled the record of charges against us and took it away by nailing it to the cross.* Thank God for Jesus!

Several years ago, I read a book by Andy Stanley entitled *Enemies of the Heart*. One chapter of the book is devoted to how we process guilt. Pastor Stanley writes, "Guilt says, 'I owe you.' For example, consider the man who runs off with another woman and abandons his family. Without realizing it at the time, he has stolen something from every member of his family. Now in the moment, he doesn't think in terms of what he has taken. Initially, he thinks in terms of what he has gained. But the first time his little girl asks him why he doesn't love Mommy anymore; his heart is stirred. He now feels guilty. Dad owes. A debt-to-debtor relationship has been established. Have you ever noticed that you rarely see the guy who owes you $50? He just never seems to come around. If you want him, you have to go out and find him. That's the power of debt. That's the power of guilt."[1]

Those words are so true, and I would add, "That's why many people avoid church." They feel the weight of their sin. They feel they owe a debt they cannot pay. But we don't have to stay distant any longer. We can draw near to God with confidence because our debt has been paid (Hebrews 4:16, Hebrews 10:22).

In his book *All In*, Mark Batterson writes, "Why do we act as though our sin disqualifies us from the grace of God? That is the only thing that qualifies us! Anything else is a self-righteous attempt to earn God's grace. You cannot trust God's grace 99%. It's all or nothing. The problem is that we want partial credit for our salvation. Yet if we try to save ourselves, we forfeit the salvation that comes from Jesus Christ alone, by grace through faith."[2]

In 2012, my wife Melissa and I moved to Knoxville, Tennessee to launch the church we now pastor. Since that time, we have witnessed hundreds of people come to Christ. Every week, we see people come to Jesus. But there's something else we've witnessed. There's a cycle: people come, they hear the gospel, they open their heart to Jesus, they receive His grace, and then many of them disappear. I've watched this happen over and over again. What's frustrating to me is that I know exactly what's going on. Chances are that new believer has messed up, and as a result, they've given up. That's what Simon Peter did.

Peter was one of Jesus' disciples. Before Peter became a Christ follower, he owned a fishing business. Then he met Jesus, and Jesus called him to be a *"fisher of men."* But at some point, Peter left his calling and went back to fishing. Notice the passage below:

> *Simon Peter said, "I'm going fishing." The other disciples said, "We'll come too."*
>
> *— John 21:3*

In other words, Peter left his calling and returned to his old way of life. Peter gave up on being who God had called him to be. He turned his back on the things of God and went the other way. Now, it's important that you realize where in relationship to the resurrection this happened. If Peter had done this after the crucifixion and before the resurrection, then I would say that Peter had given up on Jesus. In essence, Peter then would have been saying, "For three and a half years I followed that guy. I thought He was the Son of God. I thought He would overthrow the Roman Empire, and I was going to be His right-hand-man. But now He's dead. I guess I wasted a few years of my life chasing that dream. I should have known better. Now what do I do? I guess I will go back to what I know best. I need to get back to work. I need to get that fishing business back up and running again."

Again, if Peter had gone back to his old way of life, after the crucifixion and before the resurrection, then I would say that Peter had given up on Jesus. But that's not what he did. Peter went back to his old way of life after the resurrection. This tells me that Peter didn't give up on Jesus, Peter gave up on himself. In his mind, he was no longer good enough to be who God called him to be. Why? Because he failed Jesus. He had done the one thing he promised he would never do: he denied the Lord. Peter and Jesus were tight. They had walked on water together. They prayed together, preached together, laughed together, and ate together. He was one of the three guys closest to Jesus during His ministry. But when push came to shove, Peter denied Him. He failed, and because of this failure, he gave up. We've all been there. Few people ever give up on Jesus, but at some point, most people give up on themselves.

Numbers 23:19 tells us that *God is not a man that He should lie, nor is He like us that He should ever change His mind.* Jesus had not changed His mind about Peter, and He will never change His mind about you. If He doesn't change His mind about you, you shouldn't change your mind about you either. Make your mind up right now to never give up. Refuse to quit.

Few people ever give up on Jesus, but at some point, most people give up on themselves. Refuse to give up.

In 1983, Pat Benatar sang a song entitled *"Love is a Battlefield."* That song might have topped the charts in its day, but I have my own song. It's called *"The Mind is a Battlefield."* When the devil wants to attack you, he will always start with your mind first. Every person alive today has an opportunity to walk with God and to do something incredible with Him; but for most of us, our mind gets in the way.

In his book entitled *Greater*, Pastor Steven Furtick of Elevation Church writes, "I strain to believe what God has said about who I am and what He's called me to be. I find over and over again, that my greatest enemy of the greater life God has for me is… me."[3] Pastor Steven is one of the most influential leaders in the church today; yet he admits that the war in his head is real.

I am a huge fan of Pastor Jentezen Franklin. If you've never read his book, *Love Like You've Never Been Hurt*, you need to. In the book he writes, "At times I have felt unqualified to preach to others because my own marriage and family were going through hell... But I have discovered an astonishing truth; God is attracted to weakness. He cannot resist when we humbly and honestly admit how much we need Him. God is not put off by our struggles. Trouble is one of God's great servants because it reminds us how much we continually need Him."[4]

Pastor Franklin is a New York Times bestselling author, an outstanding preacher, and a presidential advisor; yet he too must silence the voices of self-defeat within his head.

Ephesians chapter six lists what we refer to as "the armor of God." Verse seventeen says, "*Put on salvation as your helmet...*" Think about this statement for a moment. Why is salvation to be worn like a helmet? Why not wear faith like a helmet? Why salvation, and why wear it like a helmet? A helmet is a defensive piece of armor designed to protect your head. This tells us that our enemy always goes for the head. Our mind; our thoughts. Hell wants us to doubt our salvation, to question whether or not anything truly happened when we prayed that prayer. If hell can keep you doubting your salvation, hell can keep you from growing in your faith.

If hell can keep you doubting your salvation, hell can keep you from growing in your faith.

Let me go on a rabbit trail for a moment. Babe Ruth will forever be a legend in the game of baseball. In his major league career, he hit 714 home runs. He was a two-time All-Star selection, seven-time World-Series champion, voted athlete of the century by the Associated Press, named the greatest baseball player of the 20th century by Sports Illustrated, named the second greatest athlete of the 20th century by ESPN, and the list goes on. But before playing in the majors, he first played in the minors. In 1914, Ruth signed with the Baltimore Orioles and in forty-six games, he only hit one home run. That's right, only one. I'm sure at some point there was a voice in his head saying, "If you couldn't do it in the minors, you'll never do it in the majors." Don't let yesterday hold you back. Yesterday ended last night. Silence those condemning voices in your head. Cling to God's Word. Press into the things of God, and never quit.

God loves you more than you think He does. Stop being so hard on yourself. God is for you more than you think He is. He's not mad at you, He's mad about you.

Face To Face With Jesus

After Peter went back to his old way of living, Jesus found Peter. Jesus always finds us, doesn't He? It's hard to hide from the One who knows all things. When Jesus found Peter, he had fished all night and hadn't caught a thing, not one fish. Peter was loathing in defeat. The old life that once brought him joy wasn't working for him anymore. After experiencing the thrill of following Jesus, nothing else could satisfy.

Now, if Jesus were like me, He would have laughed as He watched Peter struggle. I would have said something like, "If you hadn't denied Me, you wouldn't be in the shape you're in right now. How does it feel being broke and empty handed? You'd have a boat full of fish if you hadn't sold Me out."

But Jesus is not like me. Instead, Jesus said, "*Cast your net out to the side.*" When Peter did, he caught a boat sinking catch. The catch was so big his boat could not contain it. Once again, Jesus was showing Peter, and us, that He wants nothing more than to help us experience life at its best. A few moments later, Peter and Jesus were face to face on the shore. Jesus didn't ask Peter why he denied Him, or if he promised to never do it again. Jesus simply asked, "*Do you love Me, Peter?*"

"*Yes Lord,*" Peter replied.

Jesus said, *"Then go be who I called you to be. Feed My sheep."*

In other words – *This is not who I've called you to be Peter. Go be what you were born to be. And don't quit.*

If you've ever felt like giving up, check out 2 Corinthians 4:1. The verse says, *"Therefore, since God in His mercy has given us this new way, we should never give up."* What is this *"new way"* Scripture is speaking of? It's Jesus. It's called the grace of God. You see, salvation is not about what you did or didn't do; it's about receiving the benefits of what Jesus has done. It's not about making promises to God; it's about clinging to the promises God made to you.

Salvation is not about what you did or didn't do; it's about receiving the benefits of what Jesus has done. It's not about making promises to God; it's about clinging to the promises God made to you.

When Peter understood that Jesus had not given up on him, everything changed. When Peter finally realized that Jesus was for him, not against him, and when he stopped disqualifying himself, everything clicked. When the Holy Spirit came on the Day of

Pentecost, Peter was there. Peter preached, and 3,000 people were saved.

In Acts chapter 3, a lame man was healed when Peter said, "*Silver and gold I do not have, but what I do have I give you: in the name of Jesus Christ of Nazareth, rise up and walk.*" Notice what happened next:

> *And he took him by the right hand and lifted him up, and immediately his feet and ankle bones received strength. So he, leaping up, stood and walked and entered the temple with them - walking, leaping, and praising God. And all the people saw him walking and praising God.*
>
> — *Acts 3:7-9*

In Acts 5, people were laying their sick relatives on the side of the road hoping that Peter's shadow would pass over them as he walked by. The goodness of God rested on Peter's life so powerfully that people in his shadow were being healed. In Acts 9, Peter prayed for a young girl who had just passed away, and the child came back to life. Peter's story is an amazing testimony of what God can do in your life if you refuse to quit. You will always win if you refuse to quit. Never give up!

A New Mind

Several years ago, I read an article on the theory of cellular memory. The theory states that memories, as well as personality traits, are not only stored in the brain but may also be stored in major organs such as the heart. The best way to understand cellular memory is to study transplant recipients.

One of the most incredible stories is that of an eight-year-old girl who received the heart of a ten-year-old girl. After her operation, she began having nightmares of a man trying to kill her. Her dreams were so vivid that she was taken to a psychiatrist who believed they were more than just dreams. It was discovered that the donor had been murdered, and the killer was still unknown. The police used the child's dreams to gain a detailed description of the murderer and of the weapon used. The killer was identified and convicted for the crime.

In 2000, Bill Wohl nearly died after suffering a heart attack. Fortunately for Bill, he received a heart transplant which ultimately saved his life. Prior to the transplant, Bill was a hard-working executive who preferred the city life rather than the great outdoors.

Following his transplant, as his health improved, he began craving the outdoors more and more. He became quite the adventure junky. He started cycling and kayaking—something he had no interest in before. One day, a song came on the radio that brought him to tears. He had no idea why he found himself crying. The song was the work of British artist Sade.

Then one day, he had the chance to meet the family of his donor. Bill discovered his donor was in fact a Hollywood stuntman named Michael Brady. Michael was an avid sportsman, an adventure junky, an outdoorsman and Sade was Michael's favorite singer.

Many heart transplant patients have talked about new desires that accompanied their new heart. One doctor concluded that transplant recipients don't just receive a new heart; they also receive new responses, new cravings, new desires, and new habits. In Ezekiel 36:26, God said that He would give us a new heart. Notice the verse below:

> *And I will give you a new heart, and I will put a new spirit in you. I will take out your stony, stubborn heart and give you a tender, responsive heart.*
> *— Ezekiel 36:26*

Jesus didn't come to make you a better person; He came to make you new. When you received Jesus as your Lord and Savior, you underwent a heart transplant. His desires become your desires; His cravings become your cravings. You are not who you used to be. You are a child of the King. You are no longer a slave to the things that once controlled your life: you are holy, blameless, chosen, and called by God. His favor is on your life. There's a winner on the inside of you. It's time to start thinking like a winner. It's time to renew your mind.

Jesus didn't come to make you a better person; He came to make you new.

After coming to Christ, I remember thinking, "There's no way I can be saved; I still have so many ungodly thoughts." Of course, I still had ungodly thoughts. I had filled my mind with trash for years. My spirit was made new, but I still had the same old mind. Your mind is like a well, and what goes in the well, comes up in the pail. Garbage in, garbage out. You can't change the output in your life until you change the input. Unless your thinking changes, nothing will ever really change. Has it ever occurred to you that except for this present moment, your life is a collection of memories? Your mind makes up 99% of your life. What you get out of your life is the result of what you put in your life, and the memories you've created. That's why renewing our minds with God's Word is so important. Imagine a cup of muddy water. If you begin pouring fresh water into the cup, the clean water will begin pushing the dirty water out. In time, the filthy water will be replaced with clean fresh water. The same is true with our mind. Ephesians 5:25, compares reading God's Word to being washed in clean water. I love how Romans chapter twelve puts it. Notice the passage below:

> *I beseech you therefore, brethren, by the mercies of God, that you present your bodies a living sacrifice, holy, acceptable to God, which is your reasonable service. And do not be conformed to this world, but be transformed by the renewing of your mind...*

> — *Romans 12:1-2*

Think of the word "conformed" as two words: *conned* and *formed*. Don't allow the enemy to con you and form you into the pattern of this world. Be transformed by renewing your mind through the reading of God's Word. The real war is in your head. Life's battles are won or lost in the mind first. If the devil can get you to believe you're not saved, pretty soon you'll be acting like you're not saved. Don't internalize the enemy's lies. You need to get your thinking right, and that happens as you spend time reading God's Word. At the end of this chapter you will find some helpful Bible reading plans to get you started.

Don't internalize the enemy's lies.

Your life is a reflection of the thoughts you entertain. Change the way you think, and it will change your life. We tend to bring about what we think about. My life and yours will always move in the direction of our strongest thoughts. For example, have you ever passed someone on the interstate while the interstate was under construction? If so, you know all about the temporary concrete wall that sits way too close to the edge of the passing lane. The entire time you are attempting to pass, the concrete wall tries to suck you in. I'm sure you know what I'm talking about. It's like there's a magnet inside that thing. Do you know why it seems that way? Because life moves in the direction of the thoughts you entertain. If you focus on the concrete wall, you will drift towards the wall. Where the mind goes, the man follows.

After receiving Jesus as my Savior, I found myself constantly focused on *not* sinning. That might seem somewhat noble, but the problem was my focus was on sin. Instead of thinking on what to do, I was thinking on what *not* to do. It reminds me of a story I heard years ago, about a single middle-aged man who went to church hoping to find his soul mate. Scoping out the congregation, he noticed a beautiful lady about his age, sitting alone with her Bible open.

Seeing she didn't have on a wedding ring, he introduced himself and asked if he could sit down beside her. She politely smiled and nodded in agreement. That's when he noticed she had highlighted a verse in her Bible: *"Thou shall not kill."* He said, "Girl, why do you have to be reminded of that?" He quickly got up and moved to the other side of the auditorium.

Instead of fixating your thoughts on sin, fixate them on Him (Jesus), and who He has called you to be. You cannot rise above the pattern of your own thinking. That's why you need to keep your mind on the things of God. Spend a few minutes every day in God's Word. A great place to begin is the Gospel of John. After reading John, move on to the Book of Acts. There are thirty-one chapters in the Book of Proverbs, so read one chapter from Proverbs and one chapter from John's Gospel, starting today. There's a *30-Day Reading Plan* in the back of this book as well.

When I began walking with Jesus, my parents bought me the Bible on cassette. Back in the 80s, Sony made a portable cassette player called a Walkman. I would strap that bad boy on, put in my Bible cassette tape, and listen to God's Word while mowing the lawn. Every day, I would spend a few minutes reading my Bible as well. Within a year, it was amazing how much my thinking had changed. The same will happen for you as you study God's Word.

Your life is a reflection of the thoughts you entertain. Change the way you think, and it will change your life.

Let's Talk About The Mind For A Moment

The average adult brain weighs only three pounds, yet neurologists believe that each of us has the ability to learn something new every second of every hour of every day for the next three hundred million years. According to one professor's calculations, a person is able to store 2.5 petabytes of data to long-term memory.[1] That's equivalent to 300 million hours of television. Neurologists also know, for a fact, that our brain is not fixed; it is ever evolving. Every time you entertain a thought, it physically changes the landscape of your brain. The physical mass of your brain is literally shaped around the thoughts you entertain.

Your thoughts trigger biochemicals that work for you or against you. This is what psychologists call the psychosomatic network. The theory of the psychosomatic network asserts that your thoughts are directly connected to your emotions, and that your emotions are connected to your body and to your behavior.

For example, have you ever been telling someone about a time when someone did you dirty, and as you talk, your voice starts to shake, and your body begins to tremble? As you think about what that person did to you, your thoughts affect your emotions, and your emotions affect your body.

Fear triggers more than 1,400 known physical and chemical responses, which in turn, activate more than 30 different hormones within your body. The way you think and the thoughts you entertain impact every area of your life.

Here's why this is so important: Hell wants you to believe that God is against you. According to God's Word, satan does three things:

1. He lies (John 8:44).
2. He accuses (Revelation 12:10).
3. He deceives (2 Corinthians 11:3).

Don't let the devil con you out of being who God called you to be. That's what Paul was talking about when he said in 2 Corinthians 10:5, *"Cast down every thought that exalts itself against the knowledge of God."*

Train your mind towards the truth. God is for you! If you are in Christ, you are a new creation. The old is gone; the new has come. Write it down, think on it, and confess it out loud until you believe it. Use the faith declarations in the back of this book as a daily reminder of who you are in Christ.

My friend, Judy Cook, recently told me about a young man who went to his pastor and told him that he wanted to quit smoking. The pastor said, "Every time you take a puff, or buy a pack of cigarettes, say out loud, 'The Lord has delivered me from cigarettes. I have no desire for them anymore.'"

The young man was surprised by what the pastor said. He asked in disbelief, "You mean even if I am smoking a cigarette, you want me to say out loud, 'The Lord has delivered me?'" The pastor nodded his head and said, "Yes, that's exactly what I am telling you." Romans 4:17 says to *call things that are not as though they are*. The young man did what his pastor told him, and within a short time, he was totally delivered from the addiction. You see, that young man started training his mind toward the truth of God's Word. Galatians 5:1 says, "*It is for freedom that Christ has set us free. Stand firm, then, and do not let yourselves be burdened again by a yoke of slavery.*" Philippians 2:13 says, "*For God is working in you, giving you the desire and the power to do what pleases Him.*" When you begin declaring God's Word over your life, strongholds are broken. Things that used to hold you back begin to lose their grip. The Word works!

God Is For You

There's an age-old myth I believe many have bought into over the years. The myth that God is still holding something against us. If you believe this myth, you will allow your past to keep you from walking out the call of God in the present. Look at the following story from Matthew chapter nine:

> *Jesus climbed into a boat and went back across the lake to His own town. Some people brought to Him a paralyzed man on a mat. Seeing their faith, Jesus said to the paralyzed man, "Be encouraged, **My child**, your sins are forgiven.*
>
> *— Matthew 9:1-2*

Notice that Jesus called the man *His child*. This man was a child of God. This man loved God and had a relationship with God. With this in mind, let's continue reading:

> *But some (There will always be some) of the teachers of religious law said to themselves, "That's blasphemy! Does He think He's God?" Jesus knew what they were thinking, so he asked them, "Why do you have such evil thoughts in your hearts? Is it easier to say, 'Your sins are forgiven,' or 'Stand up and walk'? So I will prove to you that the Son of Man has the authority on earth to forgive sins." Then Jesus turned to the paralyzed man and*

*said, "Stand up, pick up your mat, and go home!" And
the man jumped up and went home!*
— Matthew 9:3-7

In the passage above, a paralyzed man is brought and laid at the feet of Jesus. Jesus looks at the disabled man and says, *"Be encouraged, My child! Your sins are forgiven."* Isn't that a strange thing to say to a disabled man? Why not lead off with something like, "Be healed! Rise up and walk!" Why lead off with, "Your sins are forgiven?" Who said anything about sin anyway? Why did Jesus say those words? I have a theory. Could it be that the guilt resulting from this man's past sins had rendered him immobile? I never want to allow what I once did to overshadow what Jesus has done. The religious community in the story questioned the man's salvation. That's what religion does. A religious mindset will keep you focused on the past and paralyzed in the present. A religious mindset will also keep you focused on your performance, not on God's grace. When it seems as though you haven't done enough, you condemn yourself. When it seems as though you have, you start condemning others.

**I never want to allow what I once did to
overshadow what Jesus has done.**

Make no mistake about it, character counts; but far too many people are waiting on personal perfection before ministry participation, and hell loves it. I don't think it's a coincidence that the Scripture in Matthew chapter nine ends with Jesus looking out on a multitude of hurting people and saying, *"Pray to the Lord of the harvest and ask that He would send laborers."* Don't be like the man in Matthew chapter nine. Don't let what you once did keep you from who God has called you to be. You are God's child. Through Christ, you and I have been made right with God. Stand up and be who God created you to be. You are holy, spotless, redeemed, righteous, chosen, refreshed, empowered, and loved.

Let's look at Romans chapter five for a moment. Notice the following passages:

> *Therefore, since we have been made right in God's sight by faith, we have peace with God because of what Jesus Christ our Lord has done for us. Because of our faith, Christ has brought us into this place of undeserved privilege where we now stand, and we confidently and joyfully look forward to sharing God's glory.*
>
> *— Romans 5:1-2*

> *So now we can rejoice in our wonderful new relationship with God because our Lord Jesus Christ has made us friends of God. When Adam sinned, sin entered the world. Adam's sin brought death, so death*

spread to everyone, for everyone sinned. Yes, people sinned even before the law was given. But it was not counted as sin because there was not yet any law to break.

— Romans 5:11-13

For Adam's sin led to condemnation, but God's free gift leads to our being made right with God, even though we are guilty of many sins. For the sin of this one man, Adam, caused death to rule over many. But even greater is God's wonderful grace and his gift of righteousness (righteousness is not something I earn, it's something I am gifted, I need only to receive it), for all who receive it will live in triumph over sin and death through this one man, Jesus Christ. Because one person disobeyed God, many became sinners. But because one other person obeyed God, many will be made righteous.

— Romans 5:16-19

Notice that sinners are sinners, *not only* because they have sinned, but also because Adam (the father of the human race) sinned, and they (we) are born with a sin nature. When you are born again, you become a new creation in Christ Jesus. You are not made right with God because of what you did or did not do. You are made right with God because of what He did and because you have received His "gift" of righteousness. When I was a sinner, doing good did not make me righteous, so now that I have received the gift of righteousness through faith in Christ, why would I think my failure to be perfect makes me unrighteous?

Christianity is not about perfection; it is about affection. Remember, verse seventeen of Romans five refers to the effect of what Christ did as being "*even greater*" than the effect of what Adam did. Because of Jesus, you and I can come boldly before the throne of grace (Hebrews 4:6).

Christianity is not about perfection; it is about affection.

As Pastor Joseph Prince puts it, "Right believing always produces right living." Believe that your sins were nailed to the cross, and that your debt was satisfied in Christ (Colossians 2:14). Believe that God loves you and wants a relationship with you (John 17:3). Believe that once you receive Christ, you are made right before God through faith (Ephesians 2:8-9). Believe that you can develop a personal relationship with God by reading His Word, worshipping in His house, and talking with Him in prayer — then watch what happens: right living will come.

You Are Seated With Christ

This week I heard something that I had to research for myself because I did not believe it when I heard it.

When you are conceived, during gestation, the first part of you to develop is not your heart or your brain; it's your butt. Before anything else, where you sit comes first. Everything begins with where you sit and develops from there. Now, I'm sure this seems a little random, but here's my thought: If you are going to be a victorious believer and walk in the victory Christ won for you at the cross, it begins with the revelation that *you are seated with Christ in Heavenly places* (Ephesians 2:6). You took this posture the moment you were born again. Your spiritual development begins with a firm grasp of this revelation and moves forward from there. So, regardless of what comes your way, don't give up. Refuse to quit. You live in a state of victory, not defeat.

Jesus said that if we would continue in His Word, we would know the truth, and the truth would set us free (John 8:31-32). What is the truth? The truth is that God loves us, that Jesus bore our sins, our shame, and our punishment on the cross so that we could be all God created us to be. Because of Christ, we can trust again, we can have peace, we can live a life of joy and confidence, knowing that we belong to Him and He has our back in every situation. Thank God for that!

Years ago, I noticed something Jesus said in the parable of the sower. This story is found in Matthew chapter thirteen:

"Listen! A farmer went out to plant some seeds. As he scattered them across his field, some seeds fell on a footpath, and the birds came and ate them. Other seeds fell on shallow soil with underlying rock. The seeds sprouted quickly because the soil was shallow. But the plants soon wilted under the hot sun, and since they didn't have deep roots, they died. Other seeds fell among thorns that grew up and choked out the tender plants. Still other seeds fell on fertile soil, and they produced a crop that was thirty, sixty, and even a hundred times as much as had been planted!
— Matthew 13:3-8*

"Now listen to the explanation of the parable about the farmer planting seeds: The seed that fell on the footpath represents those who hear the message about the Kingdom and don't understand it. Then the evil one comes and snatches away the seed that was planted in their hearts. The seed on the rocky soil represents those who hear the message and immediately receive it with joy. But since they don't have deep roots, they don't last long. They fall away as soon as they have problems or are persecuted for believing God's word. The seed that fell among the thorns represents those who hear God's word, but all too quickly the message is crowded out by the worries of this life and the lure of wealth, so no fruit is produced. The seed that fell on good soil represents those who truly hear and understand God's word and produce a harvest of thirty, sixty, or even a hundred times as much as had been planted!"
— Matthew 13:18-23*

Did you notice the correlation between understanding the gospel and maturing in the faith? Jesus said, *"The seed that fell on the footpath represents those who hear the message about the Kingdom and don't understand it. Then the evil one comes and snatches away the seed that was planted in their hearts."* Understand what happened when you cried out to Jesus. The Bible says, *"Whoever calls on the name of the Lord shall be saved."*2 Wrap your faith around the truth that you are not who you used to be. Don't allow the enemy to snatch from you what Jesus has accomplished in you. When you understand the gospel, the good news of Jesus, then according to verse twenty-three, you will go on to produce fruit; you will excel in life. Come on now!

Getting Started

Begin studying God's Word today. Set your alarm in the morning and allow yourself an extra thirty minutes to read and pray. I have designed this resource in hopes that it will encourage you as you begin your faith journey. Remember, anything that does not challenge you will never change you. Let me offer three tips to help you get started:

1. **Set a daily appointment**. It's those daily tweaks that lead you to mountain peaks. Make

a habit of starting your day in prayer and Bible study.

2. **Set a place**. Judas knew where to find Jesus because Jesus had a certain place He loved to pray. Choose your special place to study and pray.

3. **Set a plan**. I use what many call the S.O.A.P. plan. S.O.A.P. is an acronym that stands for Scripture, Observation, Application and Prayer. Our church offers several Scripture reading plans using the YouVersion Bible App, plans such as *The One Year Bible*, *The Gospels in 30 Days*, *A Month of Proverbs*, and many others. Go to acch.us/soap for more information. You'll find more on how to S.O.A.P. in the following pages.

My desire is that every believer would not just attend church, but also hear from God daily through His Word. As we read the Bible, we begin to see how God responds to things. Having daily devotions reshapes the way we think, transforms our spirit, and helps us become more like Jesus. S.O.A.P. journaling is a simple and excellent way to both record and process what God has spoken to you. It's also a great tool to use at a later time when you want to reflect on some of the gems you've received while studying His Word.

Without writing them down, you may forget those blessings and important revelations. Furthermore, while journaling is a very personal time with the Lord, you may want to share some of your daily notes with friends and family, so having a written record becomes very important. Through discussion, you may be able to look deeper into what God is speaking to you, gain new insight, and even encourage others. All you need to begin is a Bible, a pen, and a journal.

How to S.O.A.P.

S – Scripture
Using the study plan of your choice, open your Bible to the suggested reading for the day. As you read, allow God to speak to you. When you are done, look for a verse that particularly spoke to you that day, and write it in your journal.

O - Observation
What do you think God is saying to you in this passage of Scripture? Ask the Holy Spirit to teach you, and to reveal Jesus to you.

A - Application
Personalize what you have read by asking yourself how it applies to your life right now. Perhaps it is instruction, encouragement, a new promise, or correction for a particular area of your life. Write how this Scripture applies to you today.

P - Prayer

This can be as simple as asking God to help you apply this Scripture, or even a prayer for greater insight into what He may be revealing to you. Remember, prayer is a two-way conversation, so be sure to listen to what God has to say. Now, write it down.

As you set a plan and begin incorporating it into your daily life, God is going to transform your life in the best of ways. He is going to bring about such a transformation in you, and in the way you think that in the months to come, you will have to introduce yourself to yourself because you won't recognize yourself. Believe that! The rest of your life is going to be the best of your life.

A New Crew

Now that you've been made new in Christ and you are beginning to renew your mind, it's time to surround yourself with the right people. When you surround yourself with the right people, the right things begin to happen. When the wrong people leave your life, the wrong things stop happening. It's funny how that works. The bottom line is, you cannot soar with eagles if you are hanging out with turkeys. The Bible tells us to *choose our friends carefully* (Proverbs 12:26). According to Proverbs 13:20, if you walk with the wise, you will become wise. In 1 Corinthians 15:33, Scripture says, "*Do not be deceived, bad company corrupts good morals.*" That's why finding community within the local church is so important.

The book of Acts is a historical account of the first century church. One of the leading apostles was a man known by the name of Saul. After his conversion, God changed his name to Paul. That's what you call making a new start.

Before coming to Christ, Saul violently opposed the message of Jesus. He didn't believe that Jesus was the Messiah, God's Son. He participated in acts of terrorism, going to the extreme of killing Christians because of their faith in Jesus. Then Saul encountered Jesus himself on the road to Damascus, and his life was never the same. In one encounter, he went from Saul the destroyer to Paul the builder. Until that time, the message of Jesus was being preached only to the Jews. Paul took this message to the Gentile (non-Jewish) world. Paul was responsible for starting fourteen churches, and out of the twenty-seven books that make up the New Testament, Paul wrote thirteen.

But here's my thought: Paul would have never accomplished all that he accomplished had it not been for a good friend by the name of Barnabas. Barnabas was the one who saw something special in Paul. Most people were afraid to trust Paul, but Barnabas believed in him when no one else did. Barnabas was the one in the background, pushing Paul towards his destiny. We all need people in our lives who will push us toward our calling. Paul would have never become the man God called him to be without Barnabas.

Paul was a game changer, and there's a game changer inside you also. But like Paul, you cannot be all God created you to be without the help of others. You need the right people around you to become who you were created to be. You cannot reach your full potential on your own. God designed it this way. If you could, you'd be so full of pride that you couldn't stand to be in the same room with yourself. I would not have made it a month in my faith without the help of others. I know for a fact I would have never made it in ministry without the help of others.

Here's what else I know about Paul. Not only did he have someone pushing him towards his destiny, but he was doing the same for someone else. Timothy was a young man who Paul mentored and encouraged. Timothy became a pastor, and God used him greatly, but behind Timothy there was a Paul, and behind Paul, there was a Barnabas. In life, there will always be something or someone trying to pull us down. That's why we need people in our lives who will push us up. That's why the Bible says in Ecclesiastes 4:9-10, *"Two are better than one, because they have a good reward for their labor. For if they fall, one will lift up his companion. But woe to him who is alone when he falls, for he has no one to push him up."*

Let me give you something to think about: Jesus knew His calling. He knew the cross was coming. He knew He would suffer and die in our place for the sins we committed. There was no avoiding the cross. Yet in Matthew 27, as Jesus was walking out His calling, He began to collapse under the weight of the cross. A man by the name of Simon came alongside Jesus and helped Him bear the weight of the cross. Even Jesus needed someone to help Him fulfill His calling. If the Son of God, the One who holds the universe together, needed someone to help Him achieve His destiny, where does that leave you and me? Who is helping you carry your cross? Who are the people closest to you right now? Are those people pushing you towards your calling, or are they holding you back? Take a moment to answer those questions.

Temptation Always Begins With Isolation

Another reason why community is so important is that temptation always begins with isolation. James 1:14 tells us that *we are tempted when we are drawn away by our own evil desire and enticed.* Did you notice the word *when* in that passage? I cannot tell you where you will be tempted next, or even how, but I can tell you *when* it will happen. When you feel the most like walking away from the local church, that's when temptation will strike next. When you find yourself going from the front row to the back row, with your arms folded and your heart closed off, that's when temptation will strike next. When you want to talk to someone about a struggle but the voice in your head says, "Don't do that. You know you can't really trust anyone." That's when you know temptation is coming. Refuse to quit and refuse to live life alone. Proverbs 18:1 says, "*A man who isolates himself seeks his own desires; he rages against himself and against all wise judgment.*" The temptation to do life alone will always be there, but trust me, we are better together.

The late Portia Nelson was a singer, songwriter, actress and author. She portrayed the cantankerous Sister Berthe in *The Sound of Music*. She played the long-running role of nanny Rachel Gurney on the TV show *All My Children*. In 1977, she wrote a poem entitled *"There's a Hole in My Sidewalk."* The piece is more commonly referred to as *"An Autobiography in Five Short Chapters."* In my opinion, it's a story of overcoming temptation. The poem goes like this:

Chapter 1: I walk down the street. There is a deep hole in the sidewalk. I fall in. I'm lost. I'm helpless. It's not my fault. It takes forever to find a way out.

Chapter 2: I walk down the same street. There is a deep hole in the sidewalk. I pretend I don't see it. I fall in again. I can't believe I'm in the same place, but it's not my fault. It still takes a long time to get out.

Chapter 3: I walk down the same street. There is a deep hole in the sidewalk. I see it there; I still fall in. It's a habit, but my eyes are opened. It is my fault. I know where I am. I get out immediately.

Chapter 4: I walk down the same street. There is a deep hole in the sidewalk. I walk around it.

Chapter 5: I walk down a different street.

When you feel drawn away from the local church and godly community, you are walking down the wrong street. There's a hole in that sidewalk. There's a trap set, and your name is on it. Refuse to walk in that direction.

Overcoming Your Emotions

Before we go any further, let me say that there will be times in which you do not feel like going to church. There will be times when you don't feel like making the effort to invest relationally in others. However, one of the many things I'm still learning is that I cannot live my life based on feelings. That's why I fail so often at fitness. It feels good at first. I sign up for a gym membership. I get a t-shirt. I get a bumper sticker for my car. Melissa lets me buy a new pair of running shoes. Everything on the front end feels great, but somewhere around week three, there's that one day when everything in me says, "I'm not feeling it anymore." I wish I had a dollar for every person I've heard over the years say those same words about the church they attend. We cannot afford to live our life based on feelings. Don't allow your life to be a reflection of your feelings. Make your life a reflection of your convictions, not your feelings. Stay committed. Listen to your faith, not your feelings.

We are commanded to follow Jesus, not our emotions. If you allow your emotions to control your life, they will destroy your life. There will be times in which you do not feel saved. Are you going to believe your feelings, or are you going to believe the Word of God? You will not always feel like praying or studying God's Word. My late pastor, Ernest Brock, used to say, "There's only two times in which you should worship God: when you feel like it, and when you don't feel like it." You cannot live a victorious life and be led by your emotions. Over the years, I've heard so many people talk about how they feel. When you hear yourself using phrases like, "My anxiety, my depression, my pain," then you know you are allowing your emotions to take charge of your life.

Listen to your faith, not your feelings.

I realize these feelings are real, and I'm not belittling them; however, I never want to elevate my feelings above His Word. Be a Scripture led person, not an emotion led person. Stay connected when you feel like it, and stay connected when you don't feel like it.

Psalm 92:13 says, *"Those who are planted in the house of the Lord, they will flourish in the courts of their God."* If you want your faith to flourish, plant yourself in the local church. I've never claimed to have a green thumb. My knowledge of gardening is extremely limited, but I do know that if I put a plant in the ground, then uproot it every year and move it somewhere else, it is not going to flourish. Here's what else I know: if you attend church for any length of time, you will find a reason to leave. There is no such thing as the perfect church. If there was one, you shouldn't go there because you'll mess it up. Find a life-giving, Jesus-preaching, people-loving church, plant yourself there, and watch God do what only He can do in your life.

We are commanded to follow Jesus, not our emotions.

More than once in my life, I've heard people say that they were hurt by the church, and they stopped going because of what happened. We've all been hurt at some point in our life, but "The Church" has never hurt anyone. People hurt people, but "The Church" is the Bride of Christ, and His bride has never hurt a soul.

Think about the many ways in which The Church impacts society by offering help and hope. When natural disaster strikes, The Church is always the first to respond. In 369 A.D., The Church created the first hospital to care for those who could not care for themselves. To date, The Church is the single largest private provider of healthcare in history. It was the first to stand up for the rights of children, opening the first and largest orphanage system in the world. One hundred out of the first one-hundred and ten universities in America were founded as Christian institutions. Last year, our church alone served 2,112 families, giving away 152,588 pounds of food through our Grace Campus. We distributed 600 coats during the winter months, helped send Veterans to D.C. through Honor Air, and sent teen moms to summer camp to hear the message of Jesus Christ and find hope during such a scary time in their lives. We saw 244 people come to Christ in our services alone. There is nothing quite like The Church.

Where else do you go during the week where someone helps you park your car, someone else greets you at the door, another person serves you coffee, an amazing team cares for your children, you enjoy a first-class worship experience, you hear an inspiring message, and what's more, it doesn't cost you anything? Where else but at church does this happen? There is truly nothing like the local church. But regardless of how amazing a church is, the people who make up The Church still have their issues. We all do! If you don't think you have any issues, denial is your issue. You will never find a church where everyone agrees on every little doctrinal issue. You will never find a church where everyone has the same political view all the time. There's a reason why Jesus said, *"If two of you agree here on earth concerning anything you ask, my Father in heaven will do it for you."*[1] Do you know why He didn't say, *"If three of you can agree...?"* It's because in most cases you can't get three people to agree on anything. I can't get my family of four to agree on where to eat on Sunday afternoon.

While we are on this topic, let me add that you will never find a perfect pastor either. I can say this because I am a pastor. No one knows me better than me, and I am still a work in progress. There is only one perfect shepherd, and that's God; yet Lucifer and a third of the angels found fault with Him. The devil will work overtime to keep you away from God's house. Stay planted!

I'm reminded of a story I heard once about a man who was driving down a country road. As he neared an upcoming bridge, it appeared as though a man was preparing to jump and take his own life. Pulling onto the bridge, the driver stopped his car, jumped out and shouted, "Don't do it!"

The suicidal man said, "I don't want to live anymore. No one loves me."

The good Samaritan said, "God loves you. Do you believe in God?"

The man said, "Yes."

He asked, "Are you a Christian or a Jew?"

The man replied, "A Christian."

He said, "Me, too! Are you a Protestant or Catholic?"

The man said, "Protestant."

He said, "Me, too! What denomination?"

The man answered, "Baptist."

He said, "Me, too! Northern Baptist or Southern Baptist?"

The man said, "Northern Baptist."

He said, "Me, too! Northern Conservative Baptist or Northern Liberal Baptist?"

The man responded, "Northern Conservative Baptist."

He said, "Me, too! Northern Conservative Baptist Great Lakes Region, or Northern Conservative Baptist Eastern Region?"

The man said, "Northern Conservative Baptist Great Lakes Region."

He said, "Me, too! Northern Conservative Baptist Great Lakes Region Council of 1879, or Northern Conservative Baptist Great Lakes Region Council of 1912?"

The man said, "Northern Conservative Baptist Great Lakes Region Council of 1912."

He said, "Die, you heretic!" And he pushed him off the bridge.

You will never find a church where everyone thinks just like you about everything all the time, but that's one of the things that makes the church so incredible. The Bible compares it to iron sharpening iron. That's why at A Church Called Home we say, "In the essentials we unite, in the nonessentials we are tolerant, and in all things we love." Focus on what unites us, not on what divides us.

Shortly after Melissa and I were married, we went out one night for pizza. Some bad marinara nearly cost me my life. Within an hour, I was hugging the toilet and begging God to take me home. The next day, I was hurting from head to toe. That small-town pizza dive put a hurting on me, but you know what? I didn't stop eating. I didn't give up on food, or even pizza for that matter. Part of maturing in our faith is developing a hard to hurt attitude towards others. Make a choice to be someone who's hard to offend. Put yourself out there relationally and get connected. Sure, we all take a risk when we do that, but it's a risk worth taking. You need the local church, and the local church needs you. Refuse to do life alone. We are better together.

Three things will determine what your life looks like five years from now:

1. What you pray. Your prayer life usually becomes the script of your life, so pray big.

2. What you read, watch and listen to. What you get out of life is the result of what you put into your life.

3. The people you hang out with.

Isolation Is Deadly

Community also impacts our personal health and well-being. According to research, substance abuse and obesity can be linked to loneliness and isolation. Living a disconnected life apart from community, leads to physical illness, cognitive decline, and early death.

Recently, the *New York Times* featured a study on loneliness, and deemed our society as experiencing a "loneliness epidemic." Imagine that. In a day in which social media occupies so much of our time, we still feel disconnected. It goes to show that communication and community are not one and the same. In the workplace, loneliness decreases performance, and affects creativity, reasoning and decision-making. Moreover, loneliness and weak social connections are associated with a reduced lifespan, similar to someone smoking fifteen cigarettes a day. We were never meant to be alone.

If you are battling an addiction, the best thing you can do is talk to a godly friend. I was somewhere around eight or nine years old when first exposed to pornography. For years I fought that battle in total isolation, and for years I lost that battle. The day I was saved was the same day I went out on a limb and talked to someone about it. The youth pastor at that church became one of my best friends. He and a couple other guys at the church became my crew, holding me accountable when I needed it the most. That was nearly thirty years ago, and I am still free today. You can overcome, but you need the help of others.

Treat your struggles the same way you would treat a bully in middle school. You don't fight that kid by yourself; you get a posse. You get a crew and gang tackle that sucker. The same is true with all life's struggles. Don't fight alone. Find your crew in God's house. There are also certain levels of healing that you will never know without the help of others. Let me show you this in Scripture.

Confess your sins unto Him and He will be faithful and just to forgive you of your sins...
— 1 John 1:9

Confess your trespasses to one another, and pray for one another, that you may be healed...
                                          — *James 5:16*

When you confess your sins to Jesus, you are forgiven. But there are certain levels of healing that only come when you get honest and real with someone you can trust. Let me ask you a question. Who knows what you're struggling with at this moment? If you are the only one who knows the war within you, it's only a matter of time before you are face down in defeat. None of us are as tough as we think we are. We need one another. Don't fight alone! At A Church Called Home, we offer what we call connect groups. We believe that faith comes alive when people connect with God and with one another. Sustained life change occurs as we grow in our relationship with Christ and as we prioritize intentional relationships with others. Groups provide people with the opportunity to:

— Build life-long friendships

— Be encouraged and offer encouragement to others

— Learn from others

— Discuss questions

— Grow in your faith

Whether your church offers a clear approach to groups or not, building community is a must. Show me your friends, and I will show you your future.

When you surround yourself with the right people, the right things begin to happen.

A New Sense of Purpose

Many years ago, during my last semester of college, I read a book by Dr. Myles Munroe entitled *In Pursuit of Purpose*. Four simple words within the pages of that book left a mark on me for life. Dr. Munroe wrote, "Purpose always precedes production."

Nothing is made without there first being a purpose for it. First comes purpose, then production, and then we have the product. In Jeremiah 1:5, God said to the prophet, *"Before you were formed in your mother's womb I knew you, before you were born I set you apart, I appointed you as a prophet to the nations."* His purpose preceded his production. The same is true for you.

Let's consider for a moment how incredibly amazing God made you:

- Your eyes can see 10 million different colors, and your eye's retina makes close to 10 billion calculations every second.

- Your heart circulates 2,000 gallons of blood through 60,000 miles of blood vessels day in and day out.

- Your nose can distinguish between 10,000 odors.

- Your body is constantly inhaling oxygen, metabolizing energy, maintaining equilibrium, repairing damaged tissue, purifying toxins, digesting food, and exhaling carbon dioxide. No wonder you're so tired. You deserve a nap!

- Billions of cells in your body are being replaced every day. The lining in your intestines is replaced every 72 hours.

- Your bones are constantly going through a remodeling process. Your entire skeletal structure is replaced every ten years.

- It is believed that your liver performs in the neighborhood of 500 functions.

- Every time you laugh, your body is releasing endorphins, which act as painkillers produced by your nervous system and pituitary gland.

- You carry genetic information that is unique to you and only you. We refer to this as your DNA. A strand of DNA is six feet long. Your body contains 100 trillion strands of DNA information. This means that your body contains 600 trillion feet of DNA information. The moon is 340,649,205 feet from the earth.

If you could drive to the moon, traveling 70 mph, and never slowing down or stopping for a potty break, it would take 135 days to make a one-way-trip. However, your 600 trillion feet of DNA information, could travel to the moon and back 8,806 times. You are special in 600 trillion ways!

You are an incredible work of art and engineering.

I've always been a big Corvette fan, so several years ago, I purchased one. A few weeks later, I bought a repair manual at a local parts store. Everything I needed to know about my 1980 Corvette, I could read about in the 289 pages of that book. Yet when scientists mapped out the 3 billion codes of one human set of genes, the project filled 75,490 pages.

God did not put this kind of time and thought into you for no reason. Just like the prophet Jeremiah, God had a purpose for you long before He put you together in your mother's womb. Purpose always precedes production. Nothing is made without there first being a purpose for it. Draftsmen make an average of 27,000 sketches before a vehicle is manufactured. Every detail matters, and so it is with you. The Creator of heaven and earth meticulously handcrafted you. In Psalm 139, David said, *"You know me inside and out, You know every bone in my body; You know exactly how I was made, bit by bit, how I was sculpted from nothing into something. Like an open book, You watched me grow from conception to birth, all the stages of my life were spread out before You, the days of my life all prepared before I'd even lived one day."*

God made you on purpose for a purpose, and He made you perfect for your purpose. That's where the second half of the gospel comes in. You were saved from something, and you were saved for something.

Salvation is like a two-sided coin. On one side, you were saved from something – guilt, shame, and ultimately Hell. On the other side, you were saved for something. You were saved to fulfill your God-given purpose. Sin hindered our ability to truly walk out our purpose. Through Christ, you and I can be all we were created to be. If the cross was only about getting you to Heaven, you would have died the moment you gave your heart to Jesus. The cross was not about making us better people. The cross was *and is* about empowering us to live out our divine calling. In his book *All In*, Mark Batterson writes, "We fixate on sins of commission. Don't do this, don't do that – and you're OK. But that is holiness by subtraction. And it's more hypocrisy than holiness! It's the sins of omission – what you would have, could have and should have done – that break the heart of your Heavenly Father. How do I know this? Because I'm an earthly father! I love it when my kids don't do something wrong, but I love it even more when they do something right."[1]

As I mentioned before, when I first began my walk of faith, my focus was on not sinning. But I could avoid doing all the bad things and still fail at doing the great things God called me to do. Scripture encourages us to fix our eyes on our God given purpose. Philippians 3:14 reads, *"Press on toward the goal for the prize of the upward call of God in Christ Jesus."* You are called to be a part of something bigger than yourself. God designed you with a distinct purpose in mind.

In his book *What's Next?*, Pastor Chris Hodges writes, "What motivates you to get out of bed in the morning? How often do you feel like you were made for more? I suspect many of us feel frustrated and discontent with our lives because we're not living out the specific, unique purpose God has given us. We know there has to be more than the life we're experiencing, but we don't know how to access it. So many people work to achieve career goals and amass wealth, only to end up disappointed and disillusioned by their success. You need a sense of purpose bigger than just more money, a nicer house or the recognition of others. Because we're eternal, spiritual beings, we yearn to create an eternal, spiritual legacy."[2]

So how do you go about discovering your God given purpose? First, realize that because you are a spiritual being, you have a spiritual purpose. Walking out your purpose begins with taking your focus off the temporal things of life and placing your focus on eternal things. We see this played out in the life of Paul. His entire life was wrapped around his purpose. In Acts 20:24, he wrote, *"I consider my life worth nothing to me, my only aim is to finish the race and complete the task the Lord Jesus has given me."*

Because you are a spiritual being, you have a spiritual purpose.

The only thing that brings true contentment in life is fulfilling your God given purpose. Consider this: if everything in your life was going your way – if your finances were where you wanted them to be, if you loved your job, if everyone in your family were happy, if you lived in the home of your dreams, and if you had everything you always wanted, would you truly be content? I suspect the answer could still be no. The reason is that something very important – something essential, may still be missing. Jesus spoke of the *"deceitfulness of riches"* (Matthew 13:22). We can have all the material wealth we ever wanted, and still be missing something. It's called purpose.

Once you know your true purpose, you can then take your eyes off yourself, and focus on others. That's where your purpose really lies, in serving others and making an eternal impact in the lives of those around you. It's been widely reported that when trying out a new pen, 97% of people write their own name. This is often referred to as "The Pen Test." Deep in our subconscious, we are the first thing on our minds. Truth be told, we are all a little self-absorbed. How do I know this? Well, when you're included in a group photo, who's the first person you want to see once the picture is taken? You! We have a tendency to be "me" focused. However, Jesus taught us that greatness is found in serving others.[3] There will always be room at the top for anyone who is willing to serve. As someone once said, "The way to the throne room is through the servant's quarters."

Because Paul was so purpose-focused, his problems did not define his life. Paul had his fair share of problems: he was betrayed by his own people, beaten, left for dead, imprisoned, cold, without sleep, hungry; the list goes on. Yet, despite his many problems, Paul said, *"Therefore we do not lose heart. Though outwardly we are wasting away, yet inwardly we are being renewed day by day. For our light and momentary troubles are achieving for us an eternal glory that far outweighs them all. So, we fix our eyes not on what is seen, but on what is unseen, since what is seen is temporary, but what is unseen is eternal."*

— 2 Corinthians 4:16-18

In the face of much opposition, Paul lived a fulfilled life because he kept his eyes on his purpose. An earthly mindset will keep you focused on your problems. An eternal mindset will keep you focused on your purpose. Paul's problems did not define him or limit him because they were not his focus. I am persuaded that you and I do not need someone to solve all our problems, what we really need, is to be a part of something bigger than our problems. We need purpose.

An earthly mindset will keep you focused on your problems. An eternal mindset will keep you focused on your purpose.

At A Church Called Home, Growth Track is the on-ramp we use to get people plugged into their God-given purpose. Growth Track is a simple process designed to help people connect their gifts and passions to an eternal cause through the local church. When you connect with our Home Team and begin serving, you are literally making an eternal impact in the lives of others.

Soon after we launched A Church Called Home, I met Randy. That's not his real name, but we'll call him that anyway. After attending a few weeks, Randy decided to go through our Growth Track process. Then he began serving on one of our teams. Late one night, Randy called me. It was one o'clock in the morning to be exact. He was struggling. A few bad choices from his past had cost him several years of his life, and he was finding it difficult to start over. He was depressed and tired. We talked for quite a while that night, and during that conversation, Randy said something that I will never forget. He said, "The only reason I haven't ended my life is that I know every Sunday, I get to be a part of something bigger than what I'm going through. What I get to do each week is changing lives for eternity." That was seven years ago, and Randy is still serving today. That's the power of community. That's the power of serving. That's the power of purpose.

If your church doesn't offer a clear on-ramp to serving, jump in where you can. Ask your pastor to point you in the right direction. Since the time you were a young child on the playground during recess, you've longed to be a part of a team; we all have. Being a part of something bigger than ourselves is incredibly fulfilling. I believe that a kind greeting by a parking attendant, a friendly "welcome home" by one of our team members, or a warm cup of coffee from our café team, can be the difference maker in someone's life on any given weekend.

You Were Bought With A Price

In 2017, twenty-nine-year-old Stephen Curry signed a five-year $201 million contract with The Golden State

Warriors. You and I both know that NBA team didn't fork out that kind of money because he looks great in a blue and gold jersey. The franchise owner knew that Curry had what their team needed to win a championship. Curry averaged 25 points per game, made four straight All-Star Games, played in three straight finals, won two titles, two MVP awards, and he never misses a game. That's what makes Stephen Curry worth a $201 million dollar contract.

You need to realize that you were also purchased with a price. The Bible says, *"God bought you with a high price. So, honor Him with your life"* (1 Corinthians 6:20). You and I were purchased with the blood of Jesus (Galatians 3:13), and we were not purchased to just sit on a pew. Just as a team's owner sees gifts and talents in a player, Jesus saw something in you that was worth Him giving His life for. He purchased you with His own blood in hopes that one day, you would serve on His team. In short, you were saved to serve. Years ago, I heard someone say, "Life is like a tennis match, you'll lose if you can't serve." You were created to serve. You were saved to serve. We all were.

You were saved to serve.

The three best days of your life are: the day you were born, the day you were born again, and the day you realize why you were born and born again. Twenty-four times in the New Testament, we are referred to as *bondservants to Christ*. We were purchased to serve at His pleasure. We were purchased to make a difference. Notice the Scripture verses below:

God has reconciled us to Himself through Jesus Christ, and has given us the ministry of reconciliation.
— *2 Corinthians 5:16*

And I thank Christ Jesus our Lord who has enabled me, because He counted me faithful, putting me into the ministry.
— *1 Timothy 1:12*

But you be watchful in all things, endure afflictions, do the work of an evangelist, fulfill your ministry.
— *2 Timothy 4:5*

I think many people have a misconception of what ministry really is. Ephesians 4:11-12 says, *"Now these gifts Christ gave to the church the apostles, the prophets, the evangelists,   the shepherds and   teachers, their responsibility is to equip the saints for the work of ministry, for building up the body of Christ."* The word "ministry" in that passage simply means to serve, run errands, to assist, to be a waiter, to do the little things that others overlook. Ministry is simply doing what is needed when it's needed. Ministry doesn't start on the platform. Church doesn't begin in the auditorium. Church begins in the parking lot, at the front door, at kid's check-in, and so on. Church begins when people are greeted with a friendly smile in our café or at the connect counter. Ministry is so much more than a microphone and a platform.

My personal observation is that if your focus is a platform, you will never be satisfied. I know this because I've been there. Regardless of how large my platform has been at times, I've never been content. When ministering to hundreds, I want to minister to thousands. When ministering to thousands, I want to minister to tens of thousands. A platform focused life is a life of frustration. Nowhere in the gospels can we find Jesus placing an emphasis on platforms. Jesus called us to serve. When I keep serving as my focus, I can then be content, satisfied, and fulfilled. Let me also add that if serving is beneath me, then a platform is beyond me.

With that in mind, let's look at something Jesus taught His disciples about serving:

> But Jesus called them to Himself and said, "You know that the rulers of this world lord over their citizens, and those who are great exercise authority over the people. Yet it shall not be so among you; but whoever desires to become great among you, let him be your servant."
>
> — Matthew 20:25-26

Notice how this same story starts off in the book of Luke:

> *Now there was also a dispute among them, as to which of them was considered the greatest...*
> *— Luke 22:24*

Now look at it from Mark's perspective:

> *They came to Capernaum. When Jesus came into the house, He asked them, "What were you arguing about on the road?" But they kept quiet because on the way they had argued about who was the greatest among them. Sitting down, Jesus called the Twelve and said, "Anyone who wants to be first must be the very last, and the servant of all."*
> *— Mark 9:33-35*

Now think about this, the disciples are with Jesus and they're debating over who is the greatest among them. Here's an observation: If Jesus is in the crowd, you are not the greatest. But here's what I love about the story: Jesus didn't rebuke their desire to be great, He simply corrected their definition of what greatness really is.

They were pursuing greatness and overlooking service. We all have big dreams. We all want to do big things. However, while you and I believe for bigger things, let's not neglect the little things. If you neglect the little things, you will never do the bigger things.

Do you want to know what I look for the most in people? I look for a heart to do whatever needs to be done. Elisha was a water boy for the prophet Elijah. After Elisha was called upon to follow in the prophet's footsteps, he vanishes from Scripture for over a decade. All we know of those ten long years is that Elisha washed the hands of Elijah, but fetching water for the prophet earned him a double portion. That's the power of serving others. My friend Pastor Dan Stallbaum says, "Be faithful to your assignment, while you wait on your calling."

While you and I believe for bigger things, let's not neglect the little things.

After receiving Christ, I immediately began volunteering at my church. I mowed the lawn for several years. I cleaned the sanctuary. I cleaned the restrooms. I drove the church bus. Well, I drove the bus until I wrecked it, but that's another story. I served on the greeting team. I volunteered in the office. One weekend I served on the production team. It was my job to run the program that projected the words on the screen during worship. The problem was I'm a little ADD. Somewhere between the first and second song I drifted off in thought. The next thing I knew, the worship team had finished their last song, and the entire congregation was looking directly at me; they weren't smiling either. Did you know that volunteers can be fired from their job? They sure can, and I sure was!

The following week I volunteered to run sound, and the week after that I was fired from the sound team. Then I auditioned for the worship team. I knew I could sing. Heck, I'd been hearing myself sing for years, but no one else had ever heard me sing. One night, I mustered up the courage to audition. The entire worship team was there to observe. The soundtrack to my favorite song began, and I gave it all I had. Picture the worst audition you've ever seen on *American Idol*. That was me. Before I got to the chorus, the worship leader stood to his feet, not to congratulate me, but to stop me and to crush my dreams of ever winning a Dove Award. That night's audition was talked about, *or laughed about*, for years, but that didn't keep me from serving in other areas. I kept serving until I eventually found my niche. Jump in wherever you can and get involved. Find your thing, and give yourself entirely to it. Opportunities usually point you to your purpose. So, when you are given an opportunity to serve, go for it.

There's a God-designed reason for you being alive today, and the best place to discover it is the local church. People ask me from time to time what membership looks like at our church. For us, membership is actively participating in the ministry of Jesus; it's selling out to the cause of Christ and investing your talents and resources to moving the gospel forward. Think about gym membership for a moment. Have you ever joined a gym? By having your name in that gym's database, did it make you look any better? Did it make you feel any better? Heck no! You can join a gym, but until you start showing up and breaking a sweat, it's not working for you. That's why membership for us is not signing a document and casting a vote for the carpet sample of your choice. Membership is actively participating in the ministry of Jesus Christ, advancing the cause of Christ. That's what we were created to do.

There are some who would say, "I'm just too busy to serve." I would say, "That's one of the qualifications for serving." Busy people get things done. That's why they're so busy. Lazy people are never busy. Can you name one person in the Bible who God called who wasn't busy? Moses was tending sheep. Elisha was plowing. Rebekah was watering camels. Peter was running a fishing business. Matthew was collecting taxes. Every great man and woman in Scripture was busy when God called them. When the prophet went to Jesse's house to anoint the next king, I wonder why God chose David. Could it be because David was the only one out working? The other boys were sitting around the house. God calls busy people. Busy people make things happen.

A Final Word

Perhaps you've heard the story of Hernán Cortés, one of history's great conquistadors. He was an early settler in modern Cuba and was commissioned to explore the Mexican coastline. Instead of exploring it, he decided to conquer it. The conquest of Mexico was twofold: the first was the military conquest of the land and the people, and the second was the spiritual conquest for the Catholic Church to win the hearts and souls of that nation. You see, the Aztec Empire dominated the region. The Aztecs were known for their barbarian behavior. The act of offering human sacrifices was a norm among them. The practice was so prevalent that Cortés estimated up to four thousand people were being sacrificed every year. The Aztecs served cruel pagan gods who wanted human sacrifices in brutal fashion.

In 1519, the conquest began. One of the first things Cortés did was to order the sinking of his own ships. He did this so there would be no option for his men but to continue. This one act set an irreversible course of no retreat. There was no turning back.

Some decisions need to be made with that kind of resolve. As it should be with our decision to follow Jesus. Have a never quit attitude. Some bridges need to be burned. There's no turning back. Regardless of what comes your way, don't give up. God is for you!

The secret to succeeding at anything is our daily routines. The decisions you make today will determine the stories you tell tomorrow. As I mentioned earlier, daily tweaks set you on mountain peaks. Trust me when I tell you that the rest of your life can be the best of your life. If you will get in God's Word, spend time in daily prayer, get around the right people, discover your purpose and begin serving, you will be amazed at what God does in you and through you. Thank you for joining me. The best is yet to come!

Your Next Step

Once you've made a new start by receiving Christ, a great next step is water baptism. Baptism is an opportunity to celebrate your faith with family and friends. Being submerged in water and coming up is a picture of what's taken place in your life. The old you has died, and you have started a new life in Christ. Simply put, water baptism is an outward expression of an inward conversion. Like a wedding ring, it's the outward symbol of the commitment you made in your heart to follow Jesus.

Think about it this way: let's say you're not married at the moment and you put a wedding ring on your finger, would that make you married? No, of course not! Similarly, you can be baptized in a church, but that doesn't make you a believer in Christ. Now, what if you were married but chose not to wear your wedding ring? Would that mean you weren't married? No way, of course you would still be married. Similarly, you can be a believer in Christ, but not baptized, and your sins are still paid for and forgiven. But, if you were married, you would want the world to know that your heart belongs to your spouse. Your wedding ring testifies of that. So it is with water baptism, it's a statement to everyone watching that Christ has made you new, and you are committed to living for Him.

Why should I be baptized?
- To follow the example set by Jesus (Mark 1:9).
- Because Christ commanded it (Matthew 28:19-20).
- It's a public celebration of your faith (Acts 18:8).

What is the meaning of baptism?
- It illustrates Christ's death and resurrection (Colossians 2:12).
- It illustrates your new life in Christ (Romans 6:4).

When should I be baptized?
- As soon as you receive Christ (Acts 2:41, Acts 8:35-38).

If you've yet to be water baptized, what are you waiting for? Talk to your pastor today about taking that next step.

Bonus Material

30 Day Reading Plan on the life of Jesus

Day 1: His Birth – Luke 2:1-21

Day 2: At the Temple – Luke 2:41-52

Day 3: His Baptism – Matthew 3:13-17

Day 4: His Temptation – Luke 4:1-13

Day 5: His First Miracle – John 2:1-12

Day 6: The Sermon on the Mount – Matthew 5-7

Day 7: His Instructions – Matthew 12:16-42

Day 8: The Cost of Discipleship – Matthew 16:24-28

Day 9: Vineyard Laborers – Matthew 20: 1-16

Day 10: The Marriage Feast – Matthew 22:1-14

Day 11: Sowing Parables – Mark 4:1-34

Day 12: The Good Samaritan – Luke 10:25-37

Day 13: Prayer – Luke 11:1-13

Day 14: Lost Parables – Luke 15:1-32

Day 15: Stewardship – Luke 16:1-18

Day 16: New Birth – John 3:1-21

Day 17: The Holy Spirit – John 14:16-31, John 16:5-15

Day 18: The Good Shepherd – John 10

Day 19: The Vine and the Branches – John 15

Day 20: Lazarus – John 11

Day 21: The Triumphant Entry – Mark 11:1-11

Day 22: The Last Supper – Matthew 26:17-36

Day 23: Washing the Disciples' Feet – John 13:5-29

Day 24: Jesus Praying – John 17

Day 25: Jesus on Trial – Luke 22:47 – 23:25

Day 26: The Crucifixion – Luke 23:26-56

Day 27: The Resurrection – Luke 24:1-12

Day 28: The Road to Emmaus – Luke 24:13-35

Faith Declarations: Who You Are in Christ

I am not who I used to be (2 Corinthians 5:17).

I am not what I once did (Isaiah 54:4).

I am who God says I am, and He says I am forgiven (Psalm 103:12, Ephesians 1:7, Colossians 2:14).

He says I am chosen (1 Peter 2:9).

I am called (1 Peter 2:9).

I am royalty (1 Peter 2:9).

I am loved by God (John 3:16, Ephesians 2:4, Colossians 3:12, 1 Thessalonians 1:4).

I am an ambassador for Christ (2 Corinthians 5:20).

I am holy and without blame before Him in love (Ephesians 1:4, 1 Peter 1:16).

I have the mind of Christ, and He gives me wisdom when I ask (1 Corinthians 2:16, Philippians 2:5, James 1:5, Proverbs 2:7).

I have received the Spirit of wisdom and revelation (Ephesians 1:17-18).

I have received the power of the Holy Spirit, and I have authority over the enemy in this world (Mark 16:17-18; Luke 10:17-19).

I am fearfully and wonderfully made (Psalm 139:14).

The word of God guides me (Psalm 119:105).

Anything that touches me touches the apple of God's eye (Zechariah 2:8).

I take every thought captive and make it obedient to Christ (2 Corinthians 10:5).

Worry is not my master. I am a Word person, not a worried person (Matthew 6:25-34).

His peace guards my heart and my mind (Philippians 4:7).

God has not given me a spirit of fear, but a Spirit of power, of love, and of a sound mind (2 Timothy 1:7).

The Lord is my helper (Hebrews 13:6).

I will not be afraid. I am empowered (Colossians 1:11).

I am His masterpiece, created in Christ Jesus to do good works (Ephesians 2:10).

God's blessing is on my life (Psalm 3:8).

He daily loads me with benefits (Psalm 68:19).

His Spirit lives within me (Romans 8:11, Galatians 2:20, 1 John 4:4).

I am far from oppression, and will not live in fear (Isaiah 54:14).

I am merciful, I do not judge others, and I forgive quickly (Luke 6:36-38).

God supplies all of my needs according to His riches in glory (Philippians 4:19).

In all circumstances, I live by faith, and I extinguish all the attacks of the enemy (Ephesians 6:16).

I can do all things through Christ Jesus who gives me strength (Philippians 4:13).

In Christ, I am dead to sin - my relationship with sin is broken and I am alive in Christ- living in unbroken fellowship with Him (Romans 6:11).

Sin does not have dominion over my life (Romans 6:14).

Whom the Son has set free, is free indeed (John 8:36).

As I hear God's Word, I do what it says, and I am blessed (James 1:22, 25).

I am the righteousness of God in Jesus Christ (2 Corinthians 5:21).

I am the head and not the tail, which means, I am always ahead and never behind. I only go up and not down in life, and my best days are ahead of me (Deuteronomy 28:13).

I am free from the curse of sin, sickness, and poverty (Deuteronomy 28:15-68, Galatians 3:13).

I overflow with thanksgiving for all Christ has done for me (Colossians 2:7).

I am healed and whole because of Jesus (Isaiah 53:5, 1 Peter 2:24).

I am seated with Christ in heavenly places (Ephesians 2:5-6, Colossians 2:12).

I am strengthened with all power according to God's glorious might (Colossians 1:11).

I humbly submit myself to God, and the devil flees from me (James 4:7).

I press on each day to fulfill God's plan for my life (Philippians 3:14).

I don't break down; I break through (Psalm 144:1-3).

If God be for me, it doesn't matter who is against me (Romans 8:31).

Goodness and mercy will follow me all the days of my life (Psalm 23:6).

No one day ever defines my future (Psalm 30:5).

Times of refreshing come in the presence of the Lord (Acts 3:19).

God's favor surrounds me like a shield (Psalm 5:12).

My Heavenly Father gives me the ability to gain wealth (Deuteronomy 8:18).

He gives me joy unspeakable (1 Peter 1:8).

If tragedy strikes, there is no need to be afraid. The Lord is my confidence (Proverbs 3).

Nothing can separate me from His love (Romans 8:38).

No weapon formed against me can prosper (Isaiah 54:17).

The angels of the Lord encamp around me (Psalm 34:7).

He promises to always lead me into triumph (2 Corinthians 2:14).

He promises to complete the good work he began in me (Philippians 1:6).

He looks for an opportunity to show Himself strong on my behalf (2 Chronicles 16:9).

When disease threatens me, I know I shall live and not die (Psalm 118:17).

I am blessed!

End Notes

Chapter 1:

1. *Enemies of the Heart* by Andy Stanley, Copyright 2011, Multnomah Publishing

2. *All In* by Mark Batterson, Copyright 2013, Zondervan Publishing

3. *Greater* by Steven Furtick, Copyright 2012, Multnomah Publishing

4. *Love Like You've Never Been Hurt* by Jentezen Franklin, Copyright 2018, Chosen Books Publishing

Chapter 2:

1. Time Magazine Special Edition, The Science of Memory, November 15, 2019
2. Romans 10:13

Chapter 3:

1. Matthew 18:19

Chapter 4:

1. *All In* by Mark Batterson, Copyright 2013, Zondervan Publishing

2. *What's Next?* by Chris Hodges, Copyright 2019, Thomas Nelson Publishing

3. Matthew 23:1

About the Author

 Jason became a Christian at the age of 19. He has twenty-six years of pastoral experience serving on staff at four churches in the area of student ministry. In 2005, Jason founded a non-profit organization called Mirror-Mirror, Inc. The organization hosts events in public schools reaching tens of thousands of students across the country. Because of faithful sponsors, the organization has given over $4 million in college scholarships, and awarded students with over $14,000 in new clothing. In 2012, the Creech Family, along with a team of others, launched A Church Called Home in Knoxville, TN. Today the church offers a variety of service options to accommodate its growing congregation. Jason is also the author of the following books: *Navigate*, *Simplify*, *Pray Like You Mean It*, and *Gaining Spiritual Leverage*. He and his wife Melissa were married in 1996, and they have two wonderful children, Tori and Chaz.

Made in the USA
Columbia, SC
27 February 2024

32051359R00054